GW00496803

THE JANE HISSEY
COLLECTION

OLD BEAR
JOURNAL

EBURY PRESS STATIONERY

First published in 1991 by Ebury Press Stationery
An imprint of the Random Century Group
Random Century House, 20 Vauxhall Bridge Road,
London SW1V 2SA

Set in Horley Old Style
by FMT Graphics Limited, Southwark, London
Printed and bound in Singapore
Designed by Polly Dawes
ISBN 0 7126 4560 8

This journal belongs to

Name _____

Address _____

_____

_____

_____

Introduction

There are some ideas and thoughts which, like teddy bears, should never be thrown away or lost but treasured so that they are there when needed. You will have found a safe place to keep your bear but this journal is the place to keep your writings. In it you may put down anything you wish to remember. It might be something you have said or something you have heard, something you have hoped for or something you have achieved – a plan, a dream, a memory or an idea.

When you have written everything down and this little book is full then keep it, with your bear, for ever.

Jane Hissey

It wasn't anybody's birthday but
Bramwell Brown had a feeling that today
was going to be a special day.

Bramwell Brown suddenly remembered
that someone wasn't there who should be.

_____

_____

_____

_____

_____

_____

_____

_____

_____

_____

_____

_____

_____

_____

_____

_____

_____

_____

_____

"Never mind" said Bramwell helping
Little Bear to his feet
"We'll just have to think of something else."

"Has he been forgotten do you think?"
Bramwell asked his friends.
"I think he might have been" said Rabbit.

"Sorry" said Duck "perhaps that wasn't a very good idea." "Not one of your best" replied Bramwell from somewhere underneath the heap.

_____

_____

_____

_____

_____

_____

_____

_____

_____

_____

_____

_____

_____

_____

_____

"You never can resist a bit of bouncing" said Bramwell
"especially when it's not allowed!!!"

_____

_____

_____

_____

_____

_____

_____

_____

_____

_____

_____

_____

_____

_____

_____

_____

_____

_____

_____

_____

Rabbit and Little Bear climbed aboard and
Bramwell began the countdown "Five, four, three,
two, one, zero." They were off.

_____

_____

_____

_____

_____

_____

_____

_____

_____

_____

_____

_____

_____

_____

_____

_____

Little Bear moved a few things aside and there,
propped up against a cardboard box and covered
in dust, was Old Bear.

_____

_____

_____

_____

_____

_____

_____

_____

_____

_____

_____

_____

_____

_____

_____

_____

Little Bear jumped up and down with excitement "Old Bear, Old Bear, I've found Old Bear" he shouted. "So you have" said Old Bear.

_____

_____

_____

_____

_____

_____

_____

_____

_____

_____

_____

_____

_____

_____

_____

_____

_____

_____

_____

The others patted him too just to make him feel at home.
"It's nice to have you back" they said.

That night when all the animals were tucked up in bed,
Bramwell thought about the day's adventures and looked
at the others . . . "I knew it was going to be a special day"
he said to himself.

_____

_____

_____

_____

_____

_____

_____

_____

_____

_____

_____

_____

_____

_____

_____

_____

_____

_____

"Can boxes talk?" whispered Rabbit.
"Well this one just did" said Old Bear.
"It wasn't the box" said Old Bear,
"it was the something inside."

_____

_____

_____

_____

_____

_____

_____

_____

_____

_____

_____

_____

_____

_____

_____

_____

"Hang on" said Jolly, galloping to the
rescue, "I think I can get you down.
You can slide down my neck."

A few minutes later he returned with a carefully wrapped parcel. "It's a present for you" he said "a welcome present."

Rabbit and Duck were behind the curtains and Bramwell's feet could just be seen sticking out from under a cushion.

"I was a smart new bear once" said Rags
"but I've been hugged until I'm threadbare."

_____

_____

_____

_____

_____

_____

_____

_____

_____

_____

_____

_____

_____

_____

_____

_____

_____

_____

_____

_____

Old Bear was already enjoying the sun in his deckchair.

"I thought they were a pair of hump-warmers" said Camel
"and I tried them on to see if they fitted me."

_____

_____

_____

_____

_____

_____

_____

_____

_____

_____

_____

_____

_____

_____

_____

_____

_____

And ever since then Little Bear has slept
with his trousers under his pillow.
"Nobody will find them there" he says.

Old Bear had been busy all morning. He'd packed an
enormous picnic for all the toys. There were sandwiches,
cakes, buns, pies and jellies.

_____

_____

_____

_____

_____

_____

_____

_____

_____

_____

_____

_____

_____

_____

_____

_____

_____

"A new friend is much more fun than
a whole boxful of treasure" said Little Bear.

_____

_____

_____

_____

_____

_____

_____

_____

_____

_____

_____

_____

_____

_____

_____

"Oh dear" said Bramwell miserably "We've forgotten to have a seeker in our game of hide and seek."

"It's no good" sighed Old Bear "I can only find things
I'm not looking for."

_____

_____

_____

_____

_____

_____

_____

_____

_____

_____

_____

_____

_____

_____

_____

_____

_____

_____

_____

_____

Rabbit was just about to dive under the bed when Bramwell grabbed him by the tail.
"Wait a minute Rabbit" he said.

_____

_____

_____

_____

_____

_____

_____

_____

_____

_____

_____

_____

_____

_____

_____

_____

"It's not your fault Rabbit" said Old Bear kindly. "You were very brave to go in there on your own. . .".

_____

_____

_____

_____

_____

_____

_____

_____

_____

_____

_____

_____

_____

_____

_____

_____

There was one thing he'd always wanted to do . . . to jump into the middle of a heap of dry, crunchy autumn leaves.

_____

_____

_____

_____

_____

_____

_____

_____

_____

_____

_____

_____

_____

_____

_____

_____

_____

Then he noticed something he'd forgotten about since last year. Blackberries. Big, bright, black, juicy blackberries hanging there, just waiting to be picked.

_____

_____

_____

_____

_____

_____

_____

_____

_____

_____

_____

_____

_____

_____

_____

_____

"Oh lovely" he said as his paw touched the warm hot-water bottle. "I'm as warm as summer now."

_____

_____

_____

_____

_____

_____

_____

_____

_____

_____

_____

_____

_____

_____

_____

_____

_____

_____

"It's very disappointing" said Katie Camel "when one minute
you are in the desert and the next you're not!"

_____

_____

_____

_____

_____

_____

_____

_____

_____

_____

_____

_____

_____

_____

_____

_____

_____

_____

_____

The sun shone through the window and woke
Little Bear. "What a lovely morning" he
said to himself. "I'll do something different today."

_____

_____

_____

_____

_____

_____

_____

_____

_____

_____

_____

_____

_____

_____

_____

_____